RATTLESNAKE TALES

Written by
H. R. DeArmond

Illustrated by
Michael A. Tabangcura

White & Wilkinson

RATTLESNAKE TALES

Cover Illustration by Michael A. Tabangcura

Published in the United States of America
Modesto, California

ISBN: 978-1-7373006-3-2

Memoir

Library of Congress Control Number: 2022913971

PREFACE

I have written these stories about my adventures in the Dardanelles area of the Sierra for a couple of reasons. The first is simply that I want to share some exciting adventures that I have had in the Dardanelles area over the last many years. But my greatest reason is that this is the wild area I love beyond any other. I hope you will love it too.

The name of the area, Dardanelles, has always intrigued me. A few years ago, I took the time to discover the genesis of it. A U. S. Department of the Interior booklet describes the Dardanelles as follows:

"Part of old lava flow with several tops; thought to have been named by the J. D. Whitney survey in the 1860s because of a resemblance between the basaltic rock formations on the mountain and mountain castles which guard the Dardanelles in Turkey."*

The 1860 Whitney survey applied the name the Dardanelles to only a limited area around the cones. But in my mind, the Dardanelles area is everything from the 9,624 ft top of the Sonora Pass to just below Pinecrest Lake.

Even though I have slept in tents and on the bare mountain granite for many years; I am past my camping days now. Thankfully there are three resorts that allow me to continue my love affair with the Dardanelles. They are the Kennedy Meadows Resort, the Dardanelle Resort and the Pinecrest Lake Resort.

The Dardanelle Resort and much of the forest in the Dardanelles area was destroyed in the 2018 fire. All that remained was the 1920 era hand gas pump where I had once fueled my 1954 Ford. Thankfully, the resort, like the Phoenix, has risen from the ashes and is back in business.

The stories you are about to read all happened years ago, but a second volume is in the works; it will supply interested readers with more Dardanelles lore and some pretty interesting outdoor adventures from other parts of the world.

H. R. DeArmond

Decisions on Geographic Names in the United Sates (Decision List 7804)   Department of the Interior, Washington D.C. 1978

ACKNOWLEDGEMENTS

First and always to my wife, Jan DeArmond, for her wonderful editing assistance, but even more for her constant support and encouragement.

Many thanks to Carl Baggese for his masterful layout, editing and production assistance.

Thanks are due to Ron Wilkinson for his excellent graphic design skill and assistance.

A big shout out and thank you to Doug, Larry and the rest of the terrific staff at Athletic & Industrial Rehabilitation of Modesto. They have helped me get back on the trail more than once over these last fifteen years.

H.R. DeArmond

I would like to dedicate this book to the young and old that appreciate adventure in the outdoors.

Michael A. Tabangcura

H.R. DeArmond's recently published novel titled: THE EDUCATION OF A GRINGO details issues of immigration and education of children of migrant farmworkers during the 1960s through the 1990s. It's available online in paperback or eBook.

RATTLESNAKE TALES
PART ONE

It was early spring; trout season had just opened in the Sierra Nevada Mountains of northern California; we were going trout fishing. What a treat! Our family always made an annual trip for trout fishing in the Sierra. We usually made it later in the year when the snow melt was complete and the Stanislaus River had calmed down and returned to its rolling, transparent blue.

This year we were going early and I was as excited as any twelve year old boy could be. It was a long trek to the Dardanelles up the 1950s two-lane road, we started out early. Mom and Dad, my little brother, and our faithful Cocker Spaniel, Corky, were all going. We piled into our 1953 two-tone dark green on light green Chevrolet just after dawn and off we went. I knew that I would get car sick on that twisting, turning highway, especially the section through the town of Twain Harte. But the temporary discomfort of motion sickness was a small price to pay for the joy of being in the forest along the beautiful Stanislaus River.

Corky sat on my lap in the back seat as we rolled down the stretch of highway just outside Oakdale. He loved to hang out the window and feel the wind in his face. I held onto his collar and let him enjoy the ride as we traveled down the green tinted Highway 108 – the green color was the result of an experiment using serpentine stone as paving. Corky was a very obedient and smart dog who would have brought his head back in if I had insisted, but he loved the wind so much, I just let him feel it on his face.

It wasn't until years later that I learned how dangerous it is to let your dog hang out the window. They could lose an eye from flying objects. But Corky was never harmed and lived a long and productive life.

Corky could have joined the dog Mensa society, if there was such a thing. Once our pet parakeet escaped the cage and flew out the door to the back yard when no one was looking. All of a sudden Mom heard Corky barking furiously from the back yard. When she went to see why he was making all the ruckus, she was stunned. There was Corky holding the parakeet down on the lawn with his front paws. When she retrieved the bird, it was unharmed. Corky had somehow trapped it without doing it any harm.

Mom said Corky was really proud of himself for catching that parakeet. She thought he walked a little taller and puffed out his chest with pride. She was probably right as she was about most things. Still, I don't know if dogs really feel pride. They are probably too honorable to experience such a feeling. They just go about doing their duty with joy and no thought of any reward greater than a pat on the head. But maybe she was right. He certainly should have felt proud. I often wonder how the parakeet felt about the whole incident.

I know that Corky was a gentle dog. His treatment of the parakeet was a testament not only to his intelligence, but also demonstrated his gentle nature. Only once in my memory was he provoked to violence. Our house was on what was once farmland in Manteca, California. A variety of wild creatures had once lived there in the open fields. All of them had moved on and relocated, except the gophers. The gophers stayed and continued to do what gophers do, which is dig a pile of dirt and eat Dad's plants.

So Dad began to trap them. In the 1950s, trapping was a common way to rid residences of gophers. The traps were vile things with a pair of wire jaws that sprung up, caught, and killed the gopher. One morning Corky was making his usual inspection of every inch of the backyard to ensure that all was well. This particular morning all was not well. He discovered a gopher had been caught in a trap but had not been killed. It was still in the jaws of the trap half out of its hole. As Corky went to sniff and inspect the gopher, it rose up and bit him through the lip. Corky dispatched the gopher with a bite and shake and thereafter showed no mercy to any gopher he encountered.

Corky was descended from hunting dogs and retrievers. He loved the water. It is said that you can't teach an old dog new tricks. Maybe that's true, but in Corky's case, it wasn't. I didn't have to teach him. When I was old enough to go duck hunting, Corky was already old for a dog but I took him along anyway. I shot two ducks on that first trip, and with no training or direction from me, Corky dove into the water and retrieved them both.

I could talk about that dog all day but this is a "Rattlesnake Tale." We had finally arrived at our camping spot along the beautiful Stanislaus River, across the stream from the Dardanelle Cones. The ancient volcanic cones stood as silent sentries watching over some of the most beautiful mountains God ever created. I looked up and the sky was so incredibly blue and clear that there are no words to describe it. On this clear, crisp spring day just a few small, puffy white clouds floated lazily in a sea of pure translucent blue.

We had set up our heavy canvas tent right at the edge of the slope leading down to the river. We usually drank the water right from the river during the summer as it was so clear blue and pure in the 1950s. It was not until the widespread use of motor homes and improvement of mountain roads that the Stanislaus was overwhelmed by pollutants from the huge volume of users. On this trip the river was very high and roiled as the snow-melt water crashed down the mountain on its way to the sea. The coffee colored water was full of dirt, pine needles and various flotsam and jetsam and was undrinkable. In anticipation, we had brought our own water. Sadly, the press of human traffic in later years has made the water non-potable at all times of the year. The green moss growing on rocks in the upper Stanislaus is sad evidence of the pollutants in the water.

Across the swollen river we could see the majestic Dardanelle Cones. These spectacular extinct volcanoes are just one example of the grandeur and beauty of the Sierra Nevada Mountains. Once, on a deer hunt, Dad and I waded the river, when it was low, and climbed half way up the cones. We didn't find any deer but we did have an unexpected encounter.

We had climbed the mountain following a deer trail; the shoulder-high manzanita and buck brush clutching at us all the way. We had our WWII packs on our backs and rifles in our hands. At the end of the day, we were exhausted and looking for a place to spend the night. After searching all around, we found no place that was flat and without brush. Finally, we settled down on a bus-size flat-topped granite boulder, made a small fire, and ate our dinner of canned Spam and pork and beans.

As the night came creeping in, we rolled our sleeping bags out and crawled inside. We had no sleeping pads but the granite was cushion enough for a 16 and 35 year old. After immersing myself in the inky night sky, speckled with every star that exists in the heavens, I fell asleep.

Sometime later, I was awakened by a sound that gave me the willies. It sends a chill down my spine now as I tell the story. There we were many miles from any other human, and I heard a baby crying in the coal black night. It started with a low guttural coughing sound, "huh, huh, huh," followed by a short wailing sound like a baby crying. My first thought was that I was having a nightmare.

I asked, "Dad are you awake?"

"Yes," he replied.

"What was that noise?" I asked.

He replied, "A mountain lion."

I was more than a little nervous when I heard his answer and did not sleep too well for a while. But then one thought calmed me. We are heavily armed and mountain lions are wary of people, or at least they were in the 1950s and 60s when there was a bounty on them. And I thought, Dad had been in the battle of Okinawa and had survived. I felt safe with him. After a while, the lion moved on or at least stopped crying. We slept fitfully. In the morning we vacated the hunting grounds of that mountain lion in a hurry. Not surprisingly, we never saw a deer.

But this experience was still years in the future, and on this early spring day we were intent on catching some trout. One of the best fishing methods we had found, when the water is high and roiled, is to use a small hook baited with a worm or night crawler with a single split shot attached. Just drop it in the river and let it roll around close to the shore. This method usually produced some nice- size browns in high water. A few years later when my brother grew up a bit, he discovered a summer clear-water fishing method that was a sure fire producer of rainbows. He would use a number 0 or 1 blade Mepps spinner with no weight on it, cast across the current and just let the current carry it back toward the shore. BAM! Rainbows would hit it like silver streaking rockets.

This was spring though and Dad had found a round rock about eighteen inches high right at the water line. He was standing on the rock and busily testing each little

eddy within reach. He would drop the baited hook into the eddy, let it roll around with the water for a while, and then move the line to another spot. All this took place from his perch on the small boulder. Brother was at the camp site with Mom, and I was working my way upstream toward Dad with Corky following me.

I was walking and luxuriating in the smell of the sugar pine trees and the music of the river – so relaxing; so beautiful. All at once I was startled when Corky ran toward Dad and began to bark furiously at him. Dad continued fishing, all the while telling Corky to be quiet. I took Corky by the collar and pulled him back from the rock where Dad was fishing. But as soon as I released him he ran right back to that rock and began barking at Dad, as if a great emergency was taking place. Pulling on his collar and telling him to be quiet were of no use. He would not calm down and would not leave the area where Dad was fishing. This was very strange behavior for him; he was such an obedient and intelligent dog. Dad often said that Corky thought he was a little man with a fur coat, not a dog.

Finally, after some puzzling and consternation over this strange behavior, the cause was discovered. As I was pulling Corky away from the rock for about the fifth time, I noticed something lying right at the base of Dad's rock. It looked very much like the descriptions of banana slugs that I had read. I had never actually seen a banana slug, but I was pretty sure they didn't live in the Sierra. This creature looked, for all the world, like a huge slug. It was about nine inches long, tan in color, and uniform in size from end-to-end, a perfect geometric cylinder. I say end-to-end because there was no discernible head or tail.

"What's that by the rock?" I said.

"Where?" Dad replied.

"Right there by the bottom of the rock you're on," I shouted.

Dad stepped back off the rock and took a closer look. "I don't know," he said, "it looks like a slug".

Corky was going wild now, barking and jumping toward the rock as I held his collar to try to contain him.

Dad found a stick and pushed the slug into the water. The slug then swam out of the water in a very snake-like fashion. When it reached the shore, the slug coiled up in a very snake-like striking position. It looked like the photos I had seen of the dangerous evil snakes of the world, ready to lash out and strike some poor unsuspecting person. Without a second thought Dad killed the now newly named snake with a stick. After he had killed it, it was clearly seen as a snake, and the head was discernable. As he opened the mouth with the stick two tiny needle-like fangs could to be seen. Dad took the stick, held the body down, and caught the stick under the fangs and lifted them. They looked like two tiny strands of the monofilament fishing line that we were using. But as we knew, they were sufficient to deliver the venom stored in the now clearly visible sacs on each side of the rattlesnake's head. On further examination a tiny *button* which was the beginning of a rattle was found on the snake's tail. Dad said that these small ones were sometimes more dangerous than the big ones because they hadn't learned to limit the venom they inject.

Dad cut off the snake's head and buried it. He buried the body at a separate location not far away. He said that he had heard that sometimes the meat bees would eat a dead rattlesnake and transfer some of the venom to humans if they bit them. I don't know about that story but I was glad to see the snake underground.

That's how my first encounter with a rattlesnake ended. If it had not been for the instinct, intelligence, and persistence of a dog named Corky, this story might have had a much sadder ending for the humans involved.

RATTLESNAKE TALES
PART TWO

I was a young boy in 1953 when I took my first trip to the beautiful Sierra Nevada Mountains. Prior to that first trip, and many times after, I was schooled by my father in the dangers that might await in the mountains. There was drowning by falling in the swift moving streams, broken bones from falling off rocks, bites from meat bees, but the primary danger was rattlesnakes. Yes, a rattlesnake bite in the mid-1950s, according to our family lore, meant certain death. Well, at least a very painful and debilitating injury. I now realize that all these warnings were meant to protect, not to scare. But the result was, I went into the mountains with a tremendous fear of *rattlesnakes*!

Dad did clearly explain that rattlesnakes don't come looking for trouble. They will only strike humans when they are surprised or threatened. They prefer to retreat and hide when a creature much larger than their usual prey approaches. However, if you inadvertently step on or are close to where they hide, or worse yet, try to catch or tease one, you run the risk of being bitten.

I did not heed Dad's other warnings with nearly as much dedication as the rattlesnake warnings. I was an agile young fellow and a good swimmer. So, out of sight of my dad, I climbed a huge granite boulder that was almost vertical. In order to get to better fishing holes, I would wade out waist deep in the icy Stanislaus River. And the meat bees – I just left them alone. I did watch one, on a clear Sierra afternoon, bite chunks off a piece of salami and I could see that they could give a painful bite. But the bees and I took a live-and-let-live approach to each other.

Years later however, my brother discovered the wisdom of the bee avoidance advice. He was watching the bees buzz around and carry pine nuts and other small items of food into an underground tunnel. Being a curious lad, he decided to poke a stick into their tunnel. As you can imagine, that caused a very negative reaction from the bee society; they came boiling out and began to attack him. He then ran, swatting bees through the brush, and finally outran them.

But that was another day in the future. On this day, we set up our camp in the Dardanelles area of the Sierra. We had a big canvas tent with wooden sliding exterior poles. This particular tent was the standard in the 1950s. Campers used tents before the advent of motor homes. There were a few travel trailers and an occasional luxury Airstream. But mostly we 1950s campers slept in tents, drank cool clear water from the streams, sat around the campfire in the evening, and woke up at dawn.

After an evening of campfire marshmallow roasting and a good night's sleep, I was up and out at dawn. Mom and Dad were already up and Dad had lit the campfire. Mom had bacon frying in the pan on the Coleman stove. That was an ingenious little stove. You filled its fuel container with white gas and pumped air into it with a little plunger. It then operated the same as modern Coleman stoves operate now. The difference was that as air pressure in the old style fuel tank reduced, it had to be pumped up again, even while cooking.

Breakfast was wonderful. I always enjoyed and still enjoy bacon and eggs on a chilly mountain morning. Soon after breakfast, I was off. I was fourteen and allowed to wander the hills pretty much as I pleased. This day I had my sights set on the opposite side of the river. Some promising deep pools on the far side of the river called to me. I just knew they were full of fat rainbows.

The opposite bank was usually unapproachable. That changed during the prior winter. A huge Ponderosa Pine had fallen right across the river. It stretched, in all its fallen majesty, from bank to bank and provided a perfectly adequate bridge for a nimble fourteen-year-old.

It was to this tree bridge that I was drawn right after breakfast. The sun had just crested the Dardanelle peaks and began to warm the canyon below. I could smell the perfume of a new forest day beginning. Corky, our black and white cocker spaniel, tried to follow. He was always up for an adventure, but Dad called him back and made him stay. I know Corky must have been distressed about missing this journey, but he need not have worried; there were many future excitements in store for Corky and me.

The day was one of those beautiful clear days that I still think only occur in the Sierra Nevada. The sky was so blue, so clear and deep, that when I looked up, I felt as if I was floating in a sea of blue crystal. A few small white puffy clouds floated by on a light breeze.

I walked along the Stanislaus River among the towering, majestic Ponderosa and Sugar pines. There was a smattering of weeds and brush below the trees but the tree canopy allowed little sunlight resulting in little ground covering. I walked along, luxuriating in the beauty around me. All at once I froze. There was a strange clicking sound coming from behind a small bush at my feet. I stood stone-still, not moving a muscle, afraid at any second the snake making that noise would sink its fangs deep into my calf and inject me with its deadly venom. All my dad's warnings about the brutal dangers of rattlesnakes flashed through my mind.

I had to get out of this situation...but how? I stood there stiff as a pine sapling considering what to do. Dad had always explained that rattlesnakes don't actually leap through the air and attack as I had once imagined.

Dad said, "They must coil before they strike and can only strike about one third of their length."

With this information coursing through my anxious brain, I began to study the terrain in a circle starting at my feet and going out about five feet. I saw nothing but brush and small weeds. I decided to take a chance and move on. But as soon as I took the first step, that awful clicking started again and filled me with icy fear. It was then, as I stood frozen in fear, that I saw the source of that menacing sound—*grasshoppers*.

Yes, that's right, grasshoppers. They populated the brush and weeds in great numbers. When startled by my movement they flew, and made a strange clicking sound. As I had never actually heard a rattlesnake rattle, I mistook this sound for the dreaded rattler.

This whole episode took perhaps ten minutes, but it seemed a whole lot longer at the time. The stress of it was too much, and I had to go relieve myself behind a tree before I could continue. I did continue on though. The lure of those fat rainbows on the far side of the river was very strong. I knew that they were there and that I would have some of them in my creel before days' end.

Finally, I came to that fallen tree bridge. Its roots stuck upright now like sentries guarding the bridge crossing. As I clamored up onto the trunk, I gazed at the white water below. One slip and I would be in it and wind up down the hill in Sonora before they found me. But I was an agile young boy and had little fear of falling off the log. So up and across I went with no problem at all.

This downed tree was the kind of huge ponderosa that had almost fallen on me on a previous trip. It happened just downstream a bit. It had been a day just like this one. A beautiful blue sky, a few white puffy clouds drifting lazily by. I loved to just walk in the forest and look at the trees and bushes. I would listen to the birds, smell the forest perfume, and now and then be treated to the sight of a doe and her fawn. On that particular day the previous year, I spotted a Ponderosa Pine that seemed to stretch to the clouds. A magnificent tree, easily 200 feet tall, with a base as big around as a small car. I marched right up to that tree and stuck my nose in between two of the huge chunks on its bark. I inhaled and got a good whiff of its butterscotch scent. It smelled delicious and made my mouth water. Maybe they have butterscotch candy at the Dardanelles store or Kennedy Meadows, I thought.

It was then that I looked straight up the trunk of that Ponderosa and saw its branches thrusting out far above me. It was probably 30 feet up before the first branch began to grow. As I gazed up through its branches at the patches of blue sky, that majestic tree began to fall. I began to run for my life. I veered left then hurdled a small manzanita bush. I'm sure I ran a 10 second 100-yard dash. When I had gone what I considered a safe distance, I turned to watch the crash, but there was none. That stately tree still stretched its massive limbs to the heavens. Was I losing my mind? What had happened?

As I inched tentatively back to the tree, ready to run at the first hint of a fall, I envisioned myself squashed beneath that enormous tree trunk. But I had to know. I had to see what was happening. I reached the tree and looked up through its limbs at the blue sky. Then a cloud passed by and the tree began to fall again. Mystery solved. The movement of the cloud past the tree created the illusion that the tree was moving instead of the cloud. I have tested this illusion out on several friends over the years and 3 out of 5 will run and say that the tree is falling.

This day I crossed the log bridge and was soon following a deer trail through the buck brush with its sharp needles grabbing at my pant legs. I made my way up the riverbank to the first pool. A huge granite boulder had fallen into the riverbed. The swift water swept around it, cutting into the bank, and gouging out the soft river bottom. The result was a very deep pool of pristine blue water. I could see the bottom – it looked about three feet around and eight feet deep. It was the kind of place where trout loved to hide behind submerged rocks and wait for the current to carry food to them. I was there to accommodate them.

I had discovered that one of their favorite foods was little larvae. I'm still not sure what they were. They were about one-inch-long, encased in sand from the river bottom and attached to the rocks. These were a favorite of the Stanislaus River rainbows and I had a half can of them. I had gotten them the day before by picking them off rocks in the river. In 2015, these larvae are nowhere to be found; another sad indication of river pollution due to human activity.

I hooked a larva onto a #12 gold hook attached to my line by a four-pound test leader. I peeled off about six feet of line and tossed it upstream into the current so that it would naturally carry down and sink into the pool, where the hungry trout waited. I was not disappointed. As soon as that larva reached deep water it was snapped up and I felt the jerk on my line. Not a tentative little nibble – the trout hit that line like a runaway train. When I had brought it in I saw a gorgeous fourteen-inch rainbow. It had a brilliant rose color down its sides with all its magnificent little speckles. A beautiful, not to mention, soon to be tasty fish. I unhooked it, cracked it over the head with the back of my knife so that it didn't die slowly from asphyxiation, then dropped it on the moist leaves in my creel.

This scene was repeated nine more times in three more pools until I had my limit of ten trout. It was time to return to camp. All of them were between eight and fourteen inches and would fit nicely into Mom's frying pan at dinner that night. There was no talk of catch and release. I was fishing for dinner.

I loved to wander the woods, so I decided to take a different path back to the tree bridge. The deer and fishermen had carved out several trails in the prickly brush and I took the one a little further from the river on my way back.

I was strolling along, enjoying the day and the freedom and beauty of the woods, when I stepped over a stump in the path. To my surprise I heard a sound much like rapidly escaping air from a punctured tire. I turned to see a snake that looked the size of a dragon. It was coiled by the stump and I had almost stepped on it. I was about three feet away when it raised its head and hissed its warning at me. I saw the mouth open, and that horrible hissing noise began.

The sight of that open, hissing mouth was horrifying to me. In an instant all of the warnings about the dangers of rattlesnake bites flooded my brain. I envisioned that snake shooting out like an arrow, fangs extended, and sinking those fangs into my neck. I pictured myself flopping on the ground, writhing in pain as the life ebbed out of me. All the while, that snake would be slowly crawling away in triumph.

It was then that the flight or fight impulse took over. Needless to say, I chose the flight option. This is the only time in my life that I can say I truly panicked. I only remember brush flashing by as I sprinted as far away from that snake as I could get. Every stick along the way was another snake. In what seemed an instant, I was at the tree bridge panting and my legs were full of thorn scratches that I had not even noticed.

It was an odd and surreal feeling to have taken only minutes to cover a distance that just hours before had taken an hour of leisurely walking.

The adrenaline had dissipated enough that I could walk instead of run by the time I reached the bridge. I walked carefully over the tree bridge and back to camp. As soon as I got there I blurted out my story with a little embellishment. In this version I had almost been bitten and would have surely died on the trail.

Dad, being the calm and resolute guy he was, just picked up the Winchester 30/30 carbine that we always kept in camp and said, "Let's go take a look."

I was not anxious to go back there. I had had all the looking at that snake that I wanted. But Dad was a strong guy, and I knew I would be safe with him there. He had survived the fighting on Okinawa during WWII, and I was sure he could tackle anything we might encounter. The Winchester also gave a sense of comfort. Dad kept it in camp, not because of snakes but because there had recently been mountain lion sightings near where we camped. The lever action Winchester 30/30 held eight 150 grain hollow point bullets and was sufficient to discourage any creature with bad intentions, human or otherwise.

So we started back down the trail. Dad and I, he with the 30/30 over his shoulder and me, about ten feet behind him. We crossed over the fallen tree and made our way back up the path. As we approached the stump I hung back further, waiting to see if the monster snake would attack. The vision of its wide open mouth shining in the sun, making that horrible hiss was still fresh in my mind. That sound and the sight of the rattler remained in my consciousness for months to come.

As we approached the stump I peered around Dad and was shocked to see that the snake was gone! Oh no, he will think I made this up, I thought.

But Dad said, "The snake's gone because the sun's directly on the stump. It had to move".

I have since learned that snakes are cold-blooded creatures and have no internal temperature regulating mechanism. Consequently, they must regulate their body temperature by moving to warmer or cooler surroundings as their body requires. So the snake had gotten too warm and moved to a cooler area...but where? Was it lurking in the bushes just at our feet ready to jump out and sink its fangs into our legs? Then would it inject its deadly poison into us and leave us squirming in pain?

I know now that the image I had is not the way of rattlesnakes. They don't go looking for trouble. In fact, the reason that they rattle is to warn creatures that are not their prey, to stay away. They are actually very shy creatures and would much prefer to escape than to attack. But that was not my understanding at the time. So I stood rooted to the ground, afraid to move lest I make myself a target of those dreadful fangs.

We stood looking at every crevice and bunch of grass, but the rattler was nowhere to be seen. It was making no noise so we began to hunt for it. Today in those same circumstances, we would just consider ourselves lucky to have escaped being bitten and be on our way. But back then we were about to rid the forest of a dangerous creature that served no good purpose.

At the time it was unclear to me that rattlers, like every creature in the forest, have a place and a purpose. I have since learned that one purpose of rattlers is to keep the rodent population in check. Perhaps the people that were infected with Hantavirus in Yosemite would have been safer if a rattler had thinned out some of the virus carrying rodents.

I have also learned that the Pacific rattler is very shy. Given a choice it prefers to hide and escape from creatures too big to be food. It is a reclusive and solitary creature and will strike humans only when threatened. The fact that the human threat is not intentional is unclear to the rattler. So it will strike whenever a human is too close.

But on this day, we believed that the rattler would potentially give some other unsuspecting person a lethal bite. Thus we continued to hunt that snake to destroy it. As we came over the top of a huge grey granite boulder, there it was! The snake had moved into the shade. It had crawled under a boulder so that just its head and the upper third of its body protruded.

That's all Dad needed to see. The rattler had not yet sensed our presence. Dad slowly unslung the 30/30, rested the rifle on the boulder to steady it, and took aim. He let out half a breath so that his breathing did not throw off the shot. He slowly squeezed the trigger and then the world exploded. The sound of that rifle shot echoed from granite mountain to granite mountain and back again.

I looked up and the snake was gone. Oh no! He missed him, I thought. What will we do now? We both carefully slid down the face of our sheltering boulder and crept toward the spot where the rattler was last seen. I looked carefully in the sandy soil under the boulder. With relief, I saw its broken body. I took a manzanita stick lying near and scraped the snake out in three pieces. The hollow point 30/30 had done its destructive work. As we examined the rattler we saw that its rattles were small, dark colored and did not rattle. Dad said the snake must have shed its skin and the rattles had not yet hardened.

The snake had tried to warn me in the only way it could, by hissing. Over the years I have thought often about my experience with that snake.

RATTLESNAKE TALES
PART THREE

It was June of 1966 and I was FREE! I had just gotten my B.A. My whole life to this point, with the exception of some part-time jobs, had been going to school. Now I was free to see and engage the big world. Military service loomed in my near future. Then a profession would ensue, but not now. I was just going to enjoy the summer.

I had read Henry David Thoreau's <u>Walden</u> my last semester and was much affected by it. I decided to try out the minimalist living that he suggested, at least for a short while. I packed a fishing rod, two shiny gold trout lures, two cans of Campbell's vegetable soup and a sleeping bag. With great anticipation, I got into my 1956 Chevy Bel Air and headed for my favorite place in the world – the Dardanelles area of the Sierra Nevada Mountains. Mom was worried; Dad was skeptical; Brother and Corky wanted to go.

One early morning off I went, alone, with my minimalist supplies. My plan was to go to the woods along the Stanislaus River and live off the land. I would sleep in the car and live on water and fish from the river. In an emergency, I would eat the soup. In my twenty-two-year-old mind that was a great plan.

But my plans, as they often do, did not work out. After four days of sleeping in the car, eating campfire roasted trout washed down with cold clear Stanislaus River water, I was beginning to feel a need for a change. That was when Vern pulled up with his wife and trailer. Vern was like me in his love of the Dardanelles. He had been coming here for sixty years, since he was a boy, and he loved it. He stared lovingly at those two ancient volcanic cones we call the Dardanelles. They jut out of the brush far above the tree line in all of their black majesty. They beckon you to come and lose your cares in their deep forests and gurgling streams.

It wasn't long before Vern walked over in his Justin cowboy boots to where I sat on a rock. He invited me to dinner. He motioned to his trailer where I could see his wife stirring something in a pot. I gratefully accepted. I reasoned that even Thoreau went to Sunday dinner at Ralph Waldo Emerson's house. So this was no desertion of my minimalist plan. Vern was a friendly guy with the look of a grizzled old cowboy, my kind of guy.

Not only was Vern a friendly guy, but he was retired. Like me he had plenty of time. Unlike me, he needed a fishing partner. He had this great fishing spot down in the Stanislaus River gorge, but his wife had forbidden him to go there alone. Vern was a true believer in the saying, "A happy wife means a happy life."

It seems that a couple of years earlier he had hiked down into the canyon, a distance of about two miles with a 45-degree slope. There was no trail and the area was strewn with granite boulders and decomposed granite gravel. Vern slipped on some of the decomposed granite, fell hard against a boulder and broke his arm. Then he rolled another 20 feet downslope and came to rest just out of striking range of a large rattlesnake. The snake was startled and quickly coiled up like a tightly-wound watch spring. It struck at Vern like a bolt of lightning. Fortunately for Vern, he was out of the strike zone. As Vern's head cleared, he pulled himself further away, and the rattler retreated into a dark crevice in the granite.

Vern had the good fortune to avoid a head injury and a snake bite. But he had a badly broken arm. With the stamina developed over many years of hard work, he got himself up. He made the climb up that relentless 45-degree slope with his left arm dangling and throbbing. He later learned that it was broken in two places.

"Yeah, I don't know if I woulda made it if that snake had hit me," he said. That explained why his wife was adamant and threatening divorce if he ever went down that canyon alone again. But now he had a fishing partner – me. We were headed down the canyon in the morning. With a belly full of fried potatoes, stewed tomatoes and fried chicken, off I went to bed in my '56 Chevy. I knew I would dream of the gargantuan trout Vern promised at the bottom of the canyon.

Very early the next morning Vern drove us to the jumping off point on the canyon rim. The sun, almost cresting the Dardanelle Cones, gave a pink glow to the sky and promised warm sunlight to overcome the frigid morning. After a long and difficult walk down a boulder strewn mountain side we arrived at the Stanislaus River. Other than a few slips and stumbles, the journey was uneventful. Vern did continue to remind me that there were rattlers lurking under every rock ledge.

It's a task to remain upright when you step on a stone slab that has decomposed granite on it. The tiny crumbled pieces act like little rollers under your boots, and down you go. However, both Vern and I maintained our balance and overcame the granite ambush. We arrived at the river unharmed, unbitten, and anxious to fish.

It was a beautiful spot where the Stanislaus River rushed with the speed of a bobsled into a narrow strait which it had spent millennia cutting into the solid granite. Here the white water ceased and the river turned to a deep churning mass of azure blue, rushing on its way to be released into the waiting lake below.

The best way to fish a deep, fast-running stretch of water like this, Vern explained, was to put a little weight on the line, find an eddy in the stream, hook on a big garden worm, and let it go right to the bottom and roll around. Following his directions, I squeezed a couple of split shot onto my line. These bb-size balls were a wonderful invention! Then about two feet below the shot, I attached a #12 bait holder hook. All the tackle was provided by Vern since my new minimalist life style had left me with just two lures.

With some caution I approached the stream and found a place like Vern had described, with a little backwash caused by a submerged boulder. I flipped my line upstream to let the juicy worm be carried into the eddy and *wham*! My little trout rod bent almost double, the fight was on. After a short battle, Vern netted my beautiful 18-

inch rainbow, the first of five that day. We caught magnificent rainbow trout.

"I can't believe the size of these fish!" I shouted. Between the two of us, we caught twelve trout ranging in size from seventeen to twenty-two inches. It was probably the most glorious fishing I have ever had on the Stanislaus.

When the trout bite slowed and then came to a stop we reluctantly headed back up the canyon. The trip back up the slope was again uneventful, we arrived at the pickup just as the sun was beginning its dip below the horizon. The next day I said farewell. It had been several days of minimalist living; time to go home. I headed down the winding Highway 108 with huge trout in an ice chest Vern had loaned me.

"How will I get the chest back to you?" I asked.

"Well, I've got a lot of 'em so how about you just keep that one and bring it up here about this time next summer and we'll fill it up again," Vern replied.

"It's a deal. I'll see you right here next June," I said enthusiastically.

I kept that promise the next year and for three more years until Vern became unable to make the hike.

You can imagine the reaction when friends and family saw those fish! Everyone wanted to go to Vern's fishing hole. I had promised Vern I would only take family members there and I kept that promise. I did take one person who was not blood related, but he was and still is, as the saying goes today, "My brother from another mother (BFAM)."

A couple of weeks after my first success, my BFAM and I started out for Vern's fishing hole. However, we came to the Sierra better equipped than I had on my previous journey. Dad had loaned us his pickup with the camper on it and we had lots of fishing gear. We were young and strong and we made the hike with no issues and returned with 10 huge rainbows and no rattlesnake encounters.

It wasn't until late July that same year that my BFAM and I were able to get back together and we included Dad and my brother. Both were itching to go to Vern's special place. On a bright blue morning, just after sunrise, Dad, my little brother, and my BFAM and I started down the slope. I had passed on Vern's warning about rattlers, and everyone was watching carefully where they stepped. The boulders and crevices made ideal places for snakes to hide. We walked like ballet dancers trying not to step over a rock or ledge which might have a rattler resting on the other side.

We arrived at the river without incident and immediately began to fish. What a disappointment! In six hours of fishing we caught four rainbow trout of the usual size for the Stanislaus River – ten to twelve inches. What we did not know at the time, was that fishing at Vern's place was only good in spring and early summer when bigger rainbows moved up the river from the lake to spawn. Unlike brown trout, which spawn in the fall, rainbows spawn in the spring.

The lack of big fish in the river was a letdown. As we prepared to make the long trek back up the hill, my BFAM and I had an idea.

"Let's spend the night," I said.

"Great idea," he replied.

It was settled, we would spend the night there and fish at dawn when we were sure to get the big ones. We did not yet understand that the big fish were not in the river. They weren't back in the lake until the next spring.

Dad and Brother left us their coats for warmth during the night. BFAM and I set about making a camp. We kept the four trout that we had caught for our dinner. Fortunately, we had our own coats, too, because the pre-dawn travel to the jumping off point was very cold. The Sierra summer nights were much colder in the 1960s than in 2015.

We waved good-bye as Dad and Brother started up the hill, and then continued making camp. It was getting toward evening and we had no flashlight so we worked quickly while we still had light. We first built a fire ring of stones and cleared all pine needles and combustibles away from it. We piled up the pine needles to make beds that we would use that night and we gathered a huge pile of firewood. The best kind of campfire wood comes from the branches in rotten pine logs. The branches inside the tree are at least two to three times the circumference of the external branch and are full of sticky pitch. This pitch has nourished and protected the tree in life and now after the tree's death, it provides warmth and light to humans. We found a rotten log, kicked the branches free, and pulled out six large *pine knots*. The sharp aroma of dried pine pitch filled the air. The knots burn hot and long which was good for us because we intended to have a fire all night.

I have lived more than 70 years now, but I still remember that night of my youth with great clarity and fondness. It seemed at the time a simple thing to spend the night by the stream. But today, it still looms large in my memory as a great event. Night was coming so I made a little fire starter sandwich of pine pitch squashed between two very dry twigs. I then set it aside until just before dark when we would light the fire. Fortunately we had matches. We gathered a pile of softball size rocks and placed them next to the fire ring.

We were both hungry and the night was coming on. I lit the fire starter and placed it under the two pine knots in the fire ring. The pitch in the starter immediately began to burn like molten lava. The knots caught without hesitation, and we soon had a blazing fire. We placed the trout on forked green willow sticks and roasted our trout dinner. When the trout were nicely roasted we placed them on pieces of Ponderosa bark and ate them with wooden forks we had carved. It was a feast fit for two young adventurers.

After dinner we both went the few feet to the river and with cupped hands drank our fill. It would be a grave danger to drink from that river now. The improvement in roads, development of motor homes, and population growth in California have combined to bring many more people to the mountains. With them came pollution of the river and streams. You need only look at the Stanislaus River to verify this. The river water has a green tinge now while it once was a clear, pure blue. It now flows over moss covered rocks that were crowded with insect larvae and nothing else.

Where I once walked the pristine banks of the Stanislaus River, I now walk and pick up pounds of trash to deposit in the campground dumpsters. Not only is it unsightly, but the yards of monofilament fishing line left on the banks are a great danger. Birds and squirrels can become entangled in the line and are sometimes unable to free themselves and they die.

But back to that wonderful 1966 July day where night was falling. My BFAM and I sat on rocks and stared into the fire and told tales of adventures past and hopes for those yet to come. We talked also of bears and mountain lions and creatures that roam the night. My BFAM pulled a small semi-automatic .32 caliber pistol from his pocket and showed it to me.

"Well, here's hoping we don't need that!" I said.

Finally exhaustion took over, and we each lay down on our pile of pine needles. As I lay and gazed at a million bright stars, the Stanislaus lulled me to sleep with its sweet gurgling music. I slept like a rock except for the times when the cold drove me to get up and get a heated rock to cuddle. The round rocks we had placed near the fire were

now toasty warm. We rose at dawn, glad to see the rising sun. I remember thinking, this is how ancient man must have felt at dawn. We were glad to see the cold and dark of night whisked away by the life-giving rise of the sun.

After fishing for about two hours with nary a nibble, we gave up. The trout were not going to accommodate us. We were hungry. I stood there on a small boulder by the river and dreamed of the chocolate goodness of peanut M&Ms. But all we had for breakfast was cold, clear Stanislaus River water.

We were talking about heading up the hill when we heard my brother call out. They had come back down to fish and had pockets full of little cans of pork and beans. My BFAM and I took those cans and devoured the contents like hungry hounds. Our Spartan diet had not satisfied our young energetic bodies.

Dad and Brother wanted to fish, so bellies now full, BFAM and I lounged under a pine tree and watched the few puffy little clouds drift by in that deep endless blue sky. We sat there inhaling the intoxicating perfume of the pines and were mesmerized by the clouds. They looked like tiny ships sailing on a deep azure ocean. After a couple of hours of fishing, Dad and Brother were as disappointed as we had been, and we all decided to climb the hill back to the road.

It was a day like many days in the Sierra when the cold of night and morning begins to meld into a very warm late morning and afternoon. As we climbed out of the canyon, picking our way over and around boulders. The sun at first pleasantly warmed us and then began to make us sweat. That was the way of those Sierra days – very cold mornings would soon turn to quite hot afternoons.

The thin atmosphere at 6,000 feet not only winded you, but let in a great deal of ultraviolet light. So we took lots of shade breaks going up the hill. This accomplished the twin benefits of letting us get our breath back and to get out of the punishing sun for a while.

As we climbed, suddenly that hot day was replaced by a chill in my mind as I heard my BFAM scream *snake*! I turned to see him staggering backward over the rough terrain and pulling out his .32 pistol. In a flash he began to blast away at a snake the rest of us could not see.

We could hear though, and what we heard was the sound of metal jacketed bullets zinging off the granite rocks and boulders. Dad, Brother and I dove for cover behind boulders. Soon the firing stopped as my BFAM expended the 5 bullets in his little .32 pistol. I went over to him cautiously just in time to see him squash the head of a two-foot-long rattlesnake with a softball size rock. The snake was apparently unharmed by all the gun fire but succumbed to the blunt force trauma of a falling rock.

The rattler was a small one as rattlers go. It was about twenty inches long and had two little buttons on the end of its tail. It had been frightened by us as we came near it and was trying to escape, when my BFAM opened fire. But we had no remorse at the killing of this creature. Back then we thought we were removing a terrible menace from the woods. And to make the removal complete, we cut off the rattler's head and buried it with a pile of stones on top. The body we left for the meat bees' consumption. Then we went on our way.

RATTLESNAKE TALES
PART FOUR

It was mid-May and still very chilly in the Sierra Nevada Mountains of California. I was an old man and had pretty much limited my trout fishing to a few trips each year. This day I was not fishing, just walking and remembering.

I had chosen to take a walk around beautiful Pinecrest Lake. The lake was formed in 1914 when a dam was built to provide drinking water and generate electrical power. Now it also provides many recreational opportunities like fishing, camping, boating, and, my favorite – hiking. On this early spring day I was walking the 3.7 mile trail that rings the lake. It's a moderately difficult trail, mostly level with a few ups and downs and with beautiful lake views. Moderately difficult may be overstating the difficulty of the trail. Let me put it this way: if your grandmother ate her vegetables and didn't spend too much time in front of the television, she could probably walk it.

In any case, it is beautiful and as I crested one of the few rises on the trail, I was treated to an expansive view of the lake. On the far shore I could see small patches of snow still left from last winter's storms. Pinecrest is a small lake and from this vantage point I could see most of it. The sky was so blue, with the few puffy clouds floating by reflected in the deep crystalline lake water. It was difficult to tell sky from water.

I sat down on a gray granite boulder to rest and take in the view. But as soon as I stopped moving, memories came and with them came sorrow. It hit me like a sucker punch to the gut. I wasn't expecting it today and it almost floored me. My dog, Chips, had been my constant companion and had run this trail with me many times. Now she would be on the trail with me no longer. She lived a good full life after a bout with cancer, longer than anyone expected. She was a tough little girl, and by the grace of God, rebounded to outlive everyone's expectations. Still, her passing left a big hole in my heart. For those who have never loved a dog, this grief will be difficult to understand. But for those who have known the faithful companionship and love of a dog, no explanation is necessary.

As I tried to console myself with the knowledge that she had lived a very long life for a dog, I began to remember our life together. Chips was a thirteen pound white poodle, she was tough and fearless. The first time we went to the mountains was through the high country of Yosemite National Park, then over to the Walker River in the eastern Sierra. I parked my Nissan pickup camper and we headed for the river to pursue some of those huge Walker River rainbows. We had just reached the willow lined riverbank when she found an opening in the trees and jumped right into the white water.

I was frantic as the foaming current carried her downstream. I crashed through the thick riverside brush downstream trying to find an opening to the river to help her. When I finally was able to get to the river, about fifty yards downstream, there she was paddling around in a quiet, deep pool looking very unconcerned and enjoying her swim. That incident convinced me that she loved the water and was a good swimmer. In our many future ramblings through these mountains, she never failed to dive right into any stream or lake we passed. Thank heaven that in the future she did avoid the white water.

Pinecrest Lake was one of her favorite swimming holes even though it was very cold with snow melt until late summer. As I sat gazing up into that transparent blue sky, I remembered a time when I was waist deep in a big pool in the Stanislaus River up by the Dardanelles. I had left her on the riverbank as I waded in. Suddenly, out of the corner of my eye I saw what looked like a white duck floating by. But no, it was Chips paddling by; she had decided to join me in the middle of the Stanislaus River. I waded to shore. She followed and happily frolicked while shaking off the cold river water.

I often wonder what instinct really is. Animals are born with such innate knowledge, and we call it instinct. But it is such a wondrous thing, I'm really not sure we know what instinct is. However, instinct is the only word I have to explain how she knew which animals were potentially harmful and which were not. She had killed gophers, rats and mice. But she had only alerted me, on several occasions, of baby birds hopping around and not yet able to fly. She did not touch them, but simply followed and showed me where they went. She never saw a rattler, but I am convinced if she had, she would have warned me of the danger and known to stay away.

I finally broke away from all these sweet memories, now made sad by her passing, and walked on. As I walked the trail, my grief was lightened a bit by the thought that I still had our dog Molly at home. She was a good natured Poodle/Cairn terrier mix, and I loved her too.

Although Chips and I had been constant companions for six years, she readily accepted her two new companions, Abby and Molly. When Jan and I married, among other things Jan brought to the marriage, were her two beautiful little pups. We had the early tragedy of Abby passing at only 5 years old. Pure-breed disease was all the experts at U. C. Davis Veterinary Hospital could say.

As I walked on, my thoughts grew very morose. I began to visualize Abby's struggle for life. I remembered the helplessness we felt. I thought about the inability of even some of the greatest minds in veterinary medicine to save her life.

I thought I have to shake these painful memories. And so I walked faster and took more uphill trails in an effort to tire myself. John Muir's words, "Climb the mountains and get their good tidings. Nature's peace will flow into you," came to mind. I began to feel the truth of that statement flood my being. The pain of remembering began to ease, at least for a while, whatever the reason.

On I went up the side of a huge granite slab, through a trail in the woods and across a small bridge on a feeder stream. I saw the woods now with new eyes, and the sun seemed brighter. As I walked through a bushy part of the trail, the powdery dust kicked up and covered my boots and pant legs. The odor of the earth was calming and pure. It was then that I spotted a brownish gray object under a Manzanita bush. Some hiker must have lost their scarf, I thought.

As I got closer, I realized it was not a scarf. To my shock, I discovered that it was a tightly coiled rattlesnake. This snake was not coiled with its head up and alert as were others I had seen. It was coiled like a piece of rope, flat on the ground. I looked closer and could see no movement of any kind in the snake. It lay silent and unmoving. Is it dead? I wondered.

I stood there at a safe distance, staring at the snake for a long while. What should I do? I wondered. If I just move on and it is alive, it's right by the path and might harm someone, I thought. After some debate with myself, I decided I had to determine if it was alive. I walked back up the creek to a place where some tree branches had washed down during the spring runoff. They were piled all together like a huge tumbleweed. I found a nice long branch that would keep me at least five feet from the snake, and extricated it from the pile. Then I went back to the rattler. It had not moved and still looked dead. I moved slowly closer and poked it very gently with the stick.

There was no reaction from the rattler so I poked a little harder.

"I think I see movement," I said out loud. A third poke with the stick and the snake began to stir like a person emerging from a deep sleep. A little groggy but becoming awake. Just like me stretching and yawning, I thought. That is, if a snake can stretch and yawn. But my musings were soon disrupted as up came a fearsome looking triangular rattlesnake head. The two and a half foot long snake began to turn its head this way and that flicking its devilish forked tongue out. As that head turned and that evil looking forked tongue flicked, its tail came up and began to shake furiously. I was an old man, and my hearing was impaired enough that I couldn't hear it rattle. But swaying its head side to side, tongue flicking and tail furiously shaking...all in all, this snake presented a very fearsome looking package. It brought an innate and ancient fear up in me.

What should I do now? I can't leave an angry rattlesnake beside a path where people walk. The obvious answer was just take the stick and kill it. But that answer just wasn't good enough anymore. Somehow my primal urge to rid the world of another rattlesnake subsided. At a deep visceral level I knew it was wrong to kill it. But I couldn't leave it there by the path either. To my right, I saw a bluff with a ten foot drop to the creek shore line. That's it! I thought. I flipped and herded the snake toward the bluff. Now you may think this was easy, but herding an angry, striking, rattlesnake is no walk in the park. Finally we reached the edge of the bluff and with the stick, I helped the rattler over the edge. Down it went unharmed scrambling to a safer and, no doubt, happier place.

I have thought over the years about why I didn't kill that rattlesnake. I don't know! I'd like to think that I became enlightened and learned that rattlesnakes have an important place in the eco-system. But no, that doesn't seem to be it. More likely the struggle for life of my two beloved pets had sensitized me to the sanctity of life. I have thought, we should not needlessly destroy what we cannot create.

After all this musing on the mysteries of life, the only thing I know for sure is that this is the end of my Rattlesnake Tales.

ABOUT THE AUTHOR

H.R. DeArmond has walked the Camino de Santiago, he has hiked the French Pyrenees, the Swiss Alps, the Colorado Rockies, the Blue Ridge Mountains of Virginia, the White Mountains of Arizona and the Sierra. He has summited Mt. Whitney of California and Black Elk Peak of South Dakota. Yet he always returns to the Dardanelles area of the Sierra as his favorite. He has hiked, camped, hunted and fished there for over sixty years.

ABOUT THE ILLUSTRATOR

Michael A. Tabangcura is a self-taught artist and has enjoyed drawing since he was a boy. He works in several media; drawing with pencils and felt pens and painting with water colors and oils. He is also an accomplished wood carver. He has recently turned his hand to carving Tiki heads. He also enjoys making Christmas, birthday, business and specialty cards. His recent design for the local American Legion Women's Auxiliary pin was accepted with enthusiasm.

Notes/Sketches

Notes/Sketches

Notes/Sketches

www.ingramcontent.com/pod-product-compliance
Lightning Source LLC
Chambersburg PA
CBHW042350030426
42336CB00025B/3437